A Short History of Rome

A Short History of Rome

By

Mary Platt Parmele

Enhanced Media
2016

A Short History of Rome by Mary Platt Parmele. First published in *A Short History of Rome and Italy* by Mary Platt Parmele in 1901. This edition published 2016 by Enhanced Media.

Enhanced Media Publishing
Los Angeles, CA.

First Printing: 2016.

ISBN-13: 978-1530867073

ISBN-10: 153086707X

Contents

Chapter I

The peninsula of Italy has more powerfully influenced the destiny of the human race, in its material aspects, than any other spot upon the earth. Bethlehem of Judea and Greece have flooded the world, the one with spiritual life, and the other with intellectual splendor; but working upon a lower plane and with coarser implements, Rome seems to have been predestined to open up the channels through which those streams should nourish humanity. Her appointed task was to lay the foundations for Christendom.

But Rome did not lay the corner-stone of modern civilization. She is its corner stone. In the pedigree of nations she is the great progenitor, the cause of causes, and must ever remain the prodigy among earthly empires. What was the secret of her strength? To what was she indebted for her amazing pre-eminence? Not to her geographical position, for she had no sea-port, and in a land of exceptional fertility and charm she occupied a spot too sterile to support her own people, and was surrounded by malarial marshes unfriendly to human life. Not to her ancestry, for she had none. She did not engraft her youthful vigor upon an old pre-existing state; had not, like Persia and Macedon and Carthage, the stored riches and experience of a parent kingdom with which to build the new. We, in America, while glorying in our own phenomenal development, should remember that we are not only the heir of all the ages, but that we started with a great political inheritance, the wisdom and experience which Great Britain had been accumulating for a thousand years. But Rome first built her city, then by sheer native force peopled it, then compelled all of Italy, and finally all the then existing world, toward the centre she had created. And when after long ages her temporal sovereignty was slipping from her weakened hands, she gathered to herself a spiritual sovereignty, and remains today the supreme ruler over the hearts and consciences of a large part of mankind in an empire which knows no geographical limits. There may be great world-powers in the future, but will there ever be one which will leave such a heritage of strength and political wisdom as did that empire with its throne upon the seven hills of Rome? Will there ever be another which even while it is perishing can, out, of its superabundant strength create such a group of world-powers, and then bequeath to future ages a judicial system so just, so wise, so perfectly adapted to the needs of human society, that after 3,000 years will still stand the model for the legislation of Christendom?

In what sort of a cradle was this giant nourished? What were the influences which shaped its childhood? and what the attributes which enabled it to establish such a dominating influence in the world's affairs?

The cradle for the Roman Empire was commenced in the earliest geologic ages, and was fashioned by titanic forces. It was circumstances seemingly quite fortuitous which sent that narrow peninsula jutting out into the sea and straggling toward the East. A few more, or a few less volcanic upheavals and there would have been a different Italy, and then a different history of Rome, and hence of the world. But when Nature paused, when she had fashioned that curious leg-shaped strip of land with its rigid skeleton of mountains; when she had made it strong, rock-ribbed with her most ancient limestone, so that the elements and the sea would strive in vain to devour it, and then when she had sprinkled the depressions and basins with rich black loam which would blossom into matchless beauty beneath the sun's rays, she had determined the course of history as we read it today. And that region between the Alps and the Apennines, watered by streams from both ranges, the most fertile garden spot in Europe, was that the chosen site for the future lords of Italy and of the world? Not at all. On the Tiber, back from the sea, in the most uninviting spot in the whole peninsula, where the earth rises in seven irregular hills, there was the rough limestone cradle of the future Roman Empire.

When and how this land was first occupied by man we may never know, nor whence came the aboriginal races which existed there at the early dawn of the European day. But when it emerges from the region beyond the verge of history there were many strongly contrasting tribes crowded upon the narrow peninsula, separated from each other by the natural ramparts of the Apennines, and the no leas effectual wall of race antipathy and language. These may be roughly divided into the Pelasgians—with marked Hellenic traits — on the east and south (Magna Graecia), the Oscans, Sabellians, and Umbrians, a more indigenous people occupying Central, Western, and Northern Italy; last of all the Etruscans, on the western coast, the most interesting of the entire group, whose origin baffles even conjecture; the remains of their language offering not the slightest clew, and leaving them a companion mystery to that of the Basques in Spain and Western Europe. These are the chief primitive divisions roughly drawn. Latium, of more recent origin, seems to have been of both Pelasgian and Oscan descent; the Latin language having the same Aryan roots and structure as the Greek, but with a large vocabulary drawn from the warlike Oscans; from which facts scholars read, not that the Pelasgians and Latins were descended from the Greeks, but, as is more probable, were off-shoots of the same parent stem (Aryan) at nearly the same point, and also that at some remote period there was a conquest of the Pelasgians by the more powerful native Oscans, who then became the dominant race. How and why the Pelasgian name Italia should have gradually extended from the toe of the peninsula until it embraced the whole, may never be known. Thus far we stand upon conclusions which have the sanction of modern scholarship. But now we enter upon a more shadowy region—the region of legend and tradition, and are told that its men and women are phantoms, its facts fables, and that the fascinating narrative which has been the theme of poets and has charmed the world for two thousand years is only fiction. It was not until recently that any serious doubts were entertained of the truth of the early history of Rome. But in 1811 Niebuhr published a book of learned and searching criticism which by revealing fatal inconsistencies undermined the whole fabric. But skepticism would go too far in rejecting the only existing clews to this interesting problem. The very existence of the tradition, true or untrue, illuminates the dark and inaccessible past. It is a revelation of prehistoric hearts and character quite as genuine and of more value than the records we read in the stratifications of rocks. And however discredited we can never tear from our histories those first immortal chapters, if for no other reason than that they have been for a period which cannot be measured, an inspiration, setting before men heroic ideals of a supreme type. There was not a man in Rome, when Christ came into the world, who did not know the story of Horatius holding the bridge; nor is there a man in London or New York today who can afford not to know that immortal story. Even though it be true that Horatius the man never existed, the ideal for which he stood did; and that has a more profound significance. It matters little whether Junius Brutus did or did not hand his son over to the executioners for conspiring with the enemies of Rome. But it matters much that this was the type of civic virtue that prehistoric Rome delighted in, and this throws a flood of light upon the genesis of Roman character, and the stern, untender, uncompromising nobility of a later historic Rome. Regarding the credibility of the legends it should be remembered that in that ancient world oral tradition was unwritten history, and in a state whose very existence depended upon the truth of family traditions, it must have been cultivated as an art. The entire structure, political and social—the chief governing body, the Senate—the superior rights of the patricians—each and all alike existed by and through ancestral claims. So we may imagine that the stories upon which so much depended were endowed with an imperishable vitality. Besides this, is it not inconceivable that a political organism so coherent and consecutive, in which each step taken grew out of the one which had gone before, could have developed without accurate knowledge of legislative and historical precedents. We may not believe that Romulus was the son of Mars, nor that Egeria whispered to Numa the secret which made him the transmitter of the will of the gods. But that the main line of development is to be traced through the legendary history, we may and must believe.

Chapter II

The legendary history of Rome begins with the flight of Aeneas from the burning city of Troy, bearing upon his shoulders his old father Anchises, and leading his son Ascanius by the hand. He also carried away with him some of the sacred fire from the altar of Vesta, which must never be extinguished, for Vesta was the protectress of the race; and the gods had told Aeneas that he was going to found a mighty nation in the West. After long wanderings, described a thousand years later by Virgil, he was led to the shores of Italy. There he married Lavinia, daughter of the King of Latium, and in her honor named the city he founded Lavinium, and there he reigned over Latium and performed many mighty deeds. And when one day he disappeared, because the gods had taken him, he was worshipped as Jupiter Indiges, the god of the country. Then Ascanius (or Iulus), his son, built a new city on a ridge of the Alban hills, which he called Alba Longa, and there he reigned; and when Ascanius died, Silvius, son of Aeneas and Lavinia, also reigned there, as did eleven Silvian kings, during the next 300 years, each of them bearing the surname Silvius.

When Procas, the last of this line, died, he left two sons. The younger, Amulius, seized the inheritance, and drove away his elder brother Numitor. He then killed Numitor's son and heir, and dedicated his daughter, Rhea Silvia, to the service of Vesta, to keep alive the sacred flame brought from Troy, and be a virgin priestess forever. But although the maiden was safe from mortal lovers, the god Mars loved her, and she bore him twin boys. The penalty for her offence was to be buried alive, and when this was done, and the terrible uncle had ordered the twins to be thrown into the Tiber, he supposed the danger to his throne was past. But to fight against the gods is not easy. The basket containing Romulus and Remus floated down the Tiber, and was finally cast upon the river bank near the Palatine hill, where the babes were nourished by the historic wolf, and when they had outgrown her tender ministrations, were fed by woodpeckers, creatures forever after sacred to the Romans, and finally were sheltered and grew to young manhood, in the hut of the herdsman, Faustulus. When Numitor one day chanced to see the two young herdsmen, he was struck by their royal bearing and by their resemblance to his unhappy daughter Rhea Silvia. Then when their foster-father told him the story of their miraculous preservation in infancy, he knew they must indeed be her children; and he declared to them that he was their grandfather; and he told them of their mother and of his own wrongs at the hand of the wicked Romulus. A mighty resolve came into the hearts of the youths; that they would restore him to his throne, and overthrow the wicked usurper; which they did; and Numitor reigned at last in his own kingdom.

But Romulus and Remus were not content to stay in Alba Longa and wait for an inheritance. They determined to return to the hills on the Tiber, and there found their own city. As each desired to choose the site and to give it his name, they appealed to the gods to decide, Romulus standing upon the Palatine hill and Remus upon the Aventine, watching the heavens for an omen. The flight of six vultures over the Aventine seemed to award the choice to Remus, but a moment later twelve appeared over the Palatine, and Romulus was the chosen founder. He at once commenced to build his city, and when the envious Remus scornfully leaped over the furrow ploughed around it to mark its limits, he slew him, and was left alone to found his kingdom. When his city was ready he sent word to the neighboring tribes that all who were distressed or fugitives for any reason might find asylum there. So men fleeing from justice, slaves escaping from their masters and outcasts of all sorts found sanctuary on the Palatine, and Rome was filled with men with strong arms for its defence. Then Romulus, when the neighboring cities scornfully refused to give their daughters in marriage to outcasts and robbers, cunningly invited the Sabines, his near neighbors, to come on a certain day and witness the games in honor of a religious festival. At a given signal each man seized a maiden and bore her off. To avenge this outrage, known as "The Rape of the Sabines," the Sabine cities, of which Cures was the chief, made war upon the audacious Romans and would finally have captured their city had not the Sabine women interposed. They now loved their lords, and with dishevelled hair and cries and lamentations they rushed down the Palatine hill and threw themselves between their fathers and husbands; and there was peace, and a league was formed uniting the people of Rome and of Cures into one community; it being agreed that Romulus and the Romans should remain upon the Palatine, and to the Sabines and Tatius their king should be assigned the Quirinal, and their city be called Quirium. Hence forever after in Roman records the people are known as "Romans and Quirites." The two kings were to rule conjointly. But Tatius soon died, and Romulus reigned alone. As some of the Etruscans, his most powerful neighbors, had aided in the war with the Sabines, in reward for this they also were assigned to the Caelian hill and were given the rights of citizenship. Romulus now proceeded to organize his kingdom. He divided it into three tribes; Romans, Sabines, and Etruscans, thenceforth known as the Ramnes, Tities, and Luceres. This was the three-fold foundation for the

Roman state. Each of these main divisions he divided into ten *curiae*, and these again were composed of gentes. Or to state it more correctly, the *gens* was the family, and was the social unit. The curia was an association of families or *gentes*, and ten of these *curiae* formed the tribe, of which, as has been already said, there were three, and upon this triple foundation stood the state. These political divisions were the nucleus which, although modified, remained the core of the Roman state. Romulus then created a body composed of the fathers of the families most distinguished in the founding of Rome. These were called *patres*, because they were to the people what the father was to the gens, that is High Priest and with power of life and death, and were also an advisory Council to the King. This body was the Roman Senate, one hundred in number before the union with the Sabines, two hundred after, and later three hundred, when the third tribe (Etruscan) was represented. Then when Romulus had created a military system and divided it into centuries and legions (one century to each *curia*, the whole forming a legion), and had classified the people into two great orders, one the ruling class, and the other the inferior and dependent, he had laid the foundation for Roman institutions, political, military, and social.

As was fitting, the gods now took him, as they had his great progenitor Aeneas. During a festival on the Field of Mars, they enveloped the bills in darkness, and when the thunder and lightning ceased Romulus was gone. His father Mars had carried him to Olympus in his chariot, and he was worshipped as the god Quirinus.

So now there was no king in Rome, and for one year the fathers in the Senate took turns in reigning one after another, as interrex, each for five days, while Romans and Sabines quarrelled over the right to choose the king. Finally a compromise was agreed upon. The king was to be a Sabine, but was to be chosen by the Romans. The choice fell upon Numa Porapilius, a wise and just man. War and plunder had been until now the occupation of the people; but Numa was to change all that; not by his own but by divine power. He was beloved by the nymph Egeria, who taught him how he might compel Jupiter to reveal to him the will of the gods. At first the people would not believe that the gods spake through Numa and they mocked him. So he invited them to a simple feast. At a certain moment he told them Egeria had come to visit him; instantly the water changed to wine, the coarse food to delicious viands, and the rough benches to couches covered with rare and costly stuffs. Then they knew it was true that a divine power dwelt in Numa, and they accepted him as their king and their priest. He taught them to worship Jupiter, Mars, and Quirinus, and the sacred rites and ceremonies which must be used, the prayers, and the simple offerings of cake and milk and the fruits of the ground which the gods loved. There were to be priests to preside at the altars, but pure virgins to keep alive the sacred flame on the altar of Vesta; and he created four augurs whose duty it was to report the flight of the sacred birds, and he appointed a chief pontifex, learned in all sacred mysteries, who guarded the service and could properly construe the statutes, and save the people from incurring the wrath of the gods, through using wrong prayers or neglecting any rites. In other words, Numa gathered the diffused religious sentiment in the nation into a sacerdotal system, and if thereafter, kings and magistrates and rulers spake by authority, it was by virtue of the gods who made them the instruments for their will, and the channel for their commands.

The Temple of Janus, which was only opened in time of war, was closed during the forty-three years of Numa's reign, and all peaceful arts were encouraged, and the artisans were divided into guilds according to their occupation; and the lands conquered by Romulus were distributed among the poor; and altars erected to Terminus, the god of boundaries, and to Fides, the goddess of Faith; the one to make sacred the rights of property, and the other that honor and good faith might lie at the foundation of Society. Then, his work being done, the good Numa died, and was buried on the hill Janiculus beyond the Tiber.

Chapter III

But Tullus Hostilius, who was next chosen by the Senate, was not a lover of peace. He feared the Romans were growing effeminate and would forget how to fight. He was soon engaged in a fierce contest with the Albans. At last it became evident that either Rome would own Alba, or Alba Rome, and the issue rested upon the fate of a final battle. There chanced to be among the Romans three brothers born at one birth, the Horatii, and among the Albans three other brothers, also of the same age, named the Curiatii. It was agreed that a combat between these champions should decide the fate of the quarrel. In the presence of both armies they fought. The three Curiatii were wounded, but two of the Horatii were slain. Then, the surviving Horatius pretended to fly. Pursued by the three Curiatii the cunning Roman looked back, and when he saw his pursuers were well separated, swiftly turned upon them and slew them one at a time, gathered up their vestments, and was borne back in triumph to Rome. But his sister loved and was betrothed to one of the Curiatii, and when at sight of his blood-stained garment she wept and lamented, Horatius in a rage slew her also. The victor was condemned by the judges to be given to the executioner. But by the law of Rome he might appeal from the sentence of the Senate to the Roman people, his peers, who, because he had saved Rome, now saved her. But always afterward the Horatius gens was obliged to offer an annual sacrifice in expiation of this sin. The mighty city of Alba Longa was now destroyed, and the conquered people were compelled to come and dwell in Rome and help Tullus in his wars with Etruscans and Sabines. But the Albans were not like other strangers. Rome was founded by an Alban prince, so Tullus admitted many of the noble families into the body of the patricians, the poorer class going to swell the number of the common people. But the worship of the gods had been neglected, and when a plague broke out among the people, Tullus remembered his sin, and tried to obtain a sign from Jupiter. That wrathful god answered his prayer with lightnings, and Tullus and all his house were destroyed.

In the hope of placating heaven, Ancus Marcius, the grandson of the good Numa, was now chosen king. He was not unwilling to fight, for he conquered all of Latium between Rome and the sea, and planted a colony at the mouth of the Tiber, which he called Ostia. But he also restored the purity of the service of the gods. He fortified the hill Janiculum, where his grandsire was buried, and connected it. with Rome by a wooden bridge over the Tiber. He distributed conquered lands among the poor, and tried to follow in the footsteps of the great Numa.

The two orders into which Romulus originally divided the Roman people were composed of patrons and clients. Each of the early leading families or gentes had gathered about itself numerous servants and dependants, thus making a community of lords and vassals. The patrons, or lords, were members of the three tribes, and hence of the body-politic, while their clients had nothing whatever to do with the state except through their private relation to their lords as vassals. In the course of time these patrons, or *patricii*, came to be called patricians, as distinguished from the patres or senators. They alone could make the laws and choose the king. They were the Populus Romanus; and when the Roman people are spoken of, it is the patricians alone who are designated. Then there came into existence a third class, composed at first probably of unclassified remnants of the earliest people, swelling into great numbers chiefly through the conquest of other cities. They were freemen bat not citizens. They were unlike the clients in that they were subject to no lord or patron, and like them in that they had no connection with the state. These were the plebeians, the common people.

The two orders, patricians and plebeians, were in the very nature of things hostile to each other, and the history of their struggle is the history of early Rome. It was a struggle not for supremacy, but for equality, and every concession wrung by the plebeians from the patricians was a step toward the consummate grandeur attained by Rome; and then every encroachment upon the equality thus gained, was another step toward her final dissolution. The history of this struggle maintained for centuries with such moderation and such constancy has inscribed itself upon that model of human justice, the body of Roman law—composed of enactments wrung from the patricians; a record which finds its only counterpart in that of the British Constitution. Strangely enough in the annals of Europe it is England, with no drop of Latin blood in her veins, which most resembles the Roman state in its persistent pursuit and attainment of an equality of rights for her commons.

In a state which was growing by conquest and whose battles they fought, and in which they were numerically superior, the plebeians were politically non-existent.

Let us, if we can, imagine the descendants of the Revolutionary and Colonial families in the city of New York the ruling class, and the entire political effacement of all the rest of the people. This will give some idea of the conditions in the Roman state. It was an aristocracy of birth. The man who could not trace his lineage to the founders of the nation had not a single right of citizenship, and his connection with the state was simply by sufferance. There was still another class in Rome, which had neither rights nor freedom. These were the slaves, which had constant accessions to their numbers through conquest. The plebeians were not slaves. They were personally free; might own property and regulate their own domestic and municipal affairs in their home upon the Aventine, where they dwelt, a separate community outside of the city walls — the Ager Romanus. Intermarriage or equality of any sort, with the dwellers in the city, the patricians, was impossible. They were subject to the king, and to the laws, and must fight the battles of the common country when called upon, but with no share in the conquered lands, nor the accruing benefits to the state.

Before leaving this subject it will be interesting to note the traces of the word gens in our own language. Gentle, genteel, gentleman, are all among its descendants—and in speaking of Jews and Gentiles, it is Jews and Roman patricians that are intended. It is also helpful to know that in Roman names— usually composed of three—the first is the personal name, or *pranomen*, the second the name of the gens, the *nomen*, and the third that of the family, the *cognomen*; the nomen or *gens* always terminating in *ius*. Thus in Caius Julius Caesar, Caius is the individual name, Julius that of the Julian gens (descended from Iulus or Ascanius), and Caesar the special branch of that gens to which he belongs. Every member of the Julian gens was a Julius, and of the Cornelian and Horatian, a Cornelius or Horatius. Without understanding this, the repetition of names found in Roman history is confusing.

Chapter IV

From the mythical story of Rome we have thus far been able to read that Romulus (meaning strength) stands for the initial force which first collected the elements of the state; Numa (meaning law) for the establishing of religious and civil institutions; while the third period under Tullus and Ancus, stands for the beginning of the age of conquest, by the absorption and assimilation of neighboring tribes and peoples. Now, in the fourth and last regal period, there is introduced a foreign influence which is to be fatal. The Etruscans, hitherto a subordinate element, became the dominant race. There is not time to tell how an Etruscan refugee became King of Rome. But such was Tarquinius Priscus, who was next chosen by the Senate. The Romans and Sabines (or the Ramnes and Tities) had until now been the controlling races. The third tribe, the Luceres or Etruscans, belonged to the curiae but had never been represented in the Senate. Tarquin appointed 100 new Senators from this tribe—and also two more vestal virgins, raising the number to six. He then undertook a still more revolutionary measure. There was not an equality of condition among the plebeians. While the mass of this people was wretchedly poor, some were rich and some of noble birth in other lands. These he proposed to add to the body of patrician gentes, and in the face of fierce opposition it was done. Whatever were his motives this was in reality an assault upon the power of the nobles, and a long step had been taken toward centralizing the power of the state in the king, and converting an oligarchy into an absolute monarchy. The condition of the plebeians was unchanged and even more wretched than before, for upon them fell the task of the great public works which still exist as a memorial of this reign. At this time water filled the depressions at the foot of the Quirinal and Palatine hills. The Cloaca Maxima, the great drain which carried this body of water into the Tiber bears witness today to the power of the man who planned it and the marvellous skill of those who executed it. It was composed of three concentric arches, forming a semicircular vault fourteen feet in diameter. Its artificers were doubtless from Etruria, where similar works are still found, and so perfect was the workmanship that not a block has been displaced, and between the stones, laid without mortar or cement, it is said a knife-blade cannot be inserted, and the great cloaca performs its work as thoroughly today as it did 2,500 years ago. Upon an irregular strip of ground thus reclaimed was laid out the cattle market, or the Forum Boarium, where later were to stand the arches of Titus and of Severus, and the Temple of Saturn, of which the beautiful fragment still remains.

The Cloaca Maxima, with its ramifying branches underlying the city, also drained the valley between the Palatine and Aventine, and there Tarquin laid out a race-course, the Circus Maximus, for the chariot-races and Roman games; and on the Capitoline he laid the foundations, still existing, for the great Temple of Jupiter. But all these works were less important than his conquests in Etruria, which probably brought an influx of people from that old and exclusively aristocratic state, bringing with them social and religious usages which gave a deep and lasting coloring to those of primitive Rome. What Constantinople was at a later time to the Russians, that Etruria must have been to the Roman, who, with no ancestral splendor, was learning his first lesson in sumptuousness; for now we first hear of the lictors and their ivory chairs and purple togas, and with this elevation came the consequent degradation and misery of the class below. We learn that the plebeians, who built the great drain, were, like the Hebrews in Egypt, task-workers, and that they frequently killed themselves in despair over the tasks they were called upon to perform. And so when Tarquin the elder fell by the hand of an assassin he left a stronger and greater Rome, but one which had become a tyranny. We cannot dwell upon the circumstances which brought the good Servius to the throne. His heart seems to have been set upon alleviating the miseries of the plebeians; and, wise as well as good, he saw that this could only be done by striking at the very foundation of the social structure. The only bond uniting the entire people was a military one. Servius created a new all-embracing order, with a classification not tribal, but based upon property. In other words, he gathered all the people into a military organization; an elaborately graded system of tribes and centuries, in which the wealthiest, richly armored and with sword and spear were at the top, and the poorest, with slings and arrows, at the base. This was the Comitia Centuriata, or Assembly of the Centuries, a popular assembly which joined the plebeians to the body politic. It bestowed not power but privilege. Some of their order might now dwell within the city, and all might meet at one extremity of the Forum, while the curiae met at the other; the united bodies on occasions assembling on the Field of Mars. It was a change in the constitution freighted with immense consequences, and that it was possible for Servius so to defy and limit the authority of the aristocratic class, shows how despotic had become the kingly power during the previous reign. The chief authority had been hitherto vested in the curiae. It was the curiae which conferred upon the king his sovereignty (imperium). He could not make a single law without the consent of that body, to which also every patrician sentenced to death by the king might appeal—as did Horatius. Now, in a state always at war, and in which every man was a soldier, there had been created a Popular Assembly with entire jurisdiction over military affairs. It is easy to see that this body was destined to absorb into itself every vestige of authority, and leave the aristocratic Comitia Curiae an empty shell. Having broken down the wall of political separation, Servius then built another wall of stone and cement which girdled the seven hills, and the people on the Aventine, although not within the sacred enclosure, shared this protection from hostile attack.

According to the ancient legend the life of this benefactor terminated in a cruel tragedy. His son-in-law, the son of Tarquinius, claimed the throne by right of descent, and caused him to be slain. Tullia, the daughter of Servius, driving in her chariot to the Forum over the dead body of her father and with his blood upon her skirts, saluted her husband—"Hail to thee. King Tarquinius!" and Tarquin the Proud, Tarquinius Superbus, the last King of Rome, commenced his reign.

Unrestricted power was now in the hands of a vicious, unscrupulous king, who treated both assemblies with contempt, acknowledging no restraining authority. He compelled the people to work without pay upon the temples he was building on the Capitoline (the Capitol and Citadel), and so treacherous and insolent was he to his own order, as well as cruel to the plebeians, that when a terrible crime was committed by his son Sextus, the entire people arose to expel him. This act was a cruel outrage upon Lucretia, the daughter of a noble Roman and wife of Collatinus, who was prefect of Rome, and a cousin of the king. Lucretia sent for her father and for her husband and Lucius Brutus his kinsman, and clad in mourning garments she told them of the wrong she had suffered, and then plunged a knife into her own heart. They carried the body and the dripping knife to the Forum, and there Brutus appealed to the people to avenge this deed. With one accord they arose. King Tarquin and all of his accursed house were driven out of the city, and the gates were closed upon them. The Roman monarchy after 240 years had come to its end (493 BC).

Chapter V

The world then as now was weaving its future, and then, as it has always done, was building today upon the ruins of yesterdays. Two spiritual kingdoms had recently been planted in Asia; one in the south by Buddha, and another in the East by Confucius. The great nations of antiquity were crumbling. Babylon the mighty had just fallen. Phoenicia, old and enfeebled, was struggling with Assyria. Carthage, that vigorous young Phoenician offshoot, was extending her sturdy branches along the African coast and the Spanish Peninsula. Persia, after laying Babylonia low, was girding herself for her onslaught upon Greece; while Greece, with her brilliant cities all along the shores of the Mediterranean, was serenely moving toward her splendid meridian. Sybaris, Paestum, Cumae, Neapolis, on the Italian coast, were the abodes of fabulous luxury. What cared they whether the barbarians upon the Tiber were ruled by kings or consuls? The passing of the regal period at Rome was an event too insignificant to be observed. But Carthage, with her alert trading instincts, had even at this early day made a commercial league with the Romans, The name king had become odious to both orders. They chose two chief magistrates, who should rule for one year, and these should be called praetors, or consuls. Each should be attended by twelve lictors bearing as a symbol of power the fasces, bundles of rods, those with the projecting ends attending each consul in turn, the supreme power being vested in them alternately. The first consuls chosen were Lucius Junius Brutus and Collatinus Tarquinius, the husband of Lucretia. It was soon discovered that a band of patrician youths were plotting for the restoration of King Tarquin. When the young conspirators were brought before the consuls two sons of Brutus were among them. The stern Roman father condemned them with the rest, and himself gave the order to the lictors to scourge and then behead them with the axe. The Senate now decreed that not one of the house of Tarquin must remain in Rome, and Collatinus, the husband of Lucretia and one of the chief founders of the Republic, went into banishment with the rest of his detested name.

King Tarquin enlisted the aid of the powerful Etruscans, and many times Rome seemed nearly lost. It was to prevent complicity with these desperate attempts that there was created a new magistrate, who in times of great emergency or peril might be elected to supersede the consuls, with an absolute authority from which there should be no appeal. This was the Dictator. But consul or dictator when no longer under the official aegis might for unlawful use of authority be impeached, and suffer like any other citizen.

It was when King Porsenna, of Clusium, the champion of Tarquin, arrived with his army at the bridge across the Tiber that Horatius performed his immortal act of valor. With two others he held the entrance to the bridge while it was being broken down behind them. Just before the destruction was complete his two companions lied back to the city, but he, receiving upon his shield the rain of arrows, waited until the last plank had fallen, then fully armored, leaped into the Tiber, and swam to the opposite shore. So a second time had a Horatian saved Rome.

The last and fiercest battle at Lake Regillus was nearly lost, when suddenly there appeared two youths, on white chargers. The gods had interposed, for these were Castor and Pollux, the sacred twins. They turned the tide of victory, and the grateful Romans erected a temple for their worship in the Forum. Tarquin, wearied and disheartened, now retired to the Greek city of Cumae, and there he died.

The fourteen years of war since the expulsion of Tarquin had brought utter ruin upon the plebeians. Not alone had their farms been deserted while they fought, but lying outside the city, in the Campagna, as most of them did, they had been ravaged by hostile bands, their cattle and flocks earned off, and homesteads burned. The patricians, who had suffered none of these things, had, from time to time, loaned them money to restock their farms, and to keep them from starvation. But now that there was peace, and they no longer needed the help of the people, the mask of friendship was torn off. The time had come when their own order could be restored to its old supremacy. The Roman law of debt was of frightful severity. If the debt was not discharged at the appointed time, the creditor might sell the debtor and all his sons to the highest bidder. Or if the father preferred to spare his children such a fate, he might be put to death, his body be hewed in pieces, and distributed in proper proportion among his creditors; it being especially provided, in anticipation of some future Portia, that a little more or a little less made no difference. The plebeians found that they were becoming the bonded slaves of the patricians, on account of losses sustained in fighting their battles, and that all the rights obtained for them by Servius were trampled upon.

They resolved to bear it no longer. They solemnly marched in a body to a hill on the Tiber north of Rome. There they would build their own city and dwell, and leave the patricians and their clients and their slaves to themselves. This meant the dissolution of the Republic. There was consternation in Rome. Embassies were sent, offers of concessions made. The plebeians knew what they wanted; nothing less would satisfy them. All debts must be cancelled; those already sold into bondage must have their freedom restored; and two officials must be created in their own order, with the authority and the desire to protect them from patrician injustice. The power and the persons of these Tribunes, or masters of the tribes, were to be sacred and invio-inviolable as those of tile consuls; and in matters touching the rights of the plebeians, their jurisdiction was to extend over the patricians themselves, who could be impeached and must stand trial before the Assembly of the Tribes.

Not until the last point was yielded would the determined seceders sign the treaty; and the hill where this solemn league was made was forever called the *Mons Sacre* or Sacred Hill. The bestowal of the power to arrest legislation shows how desperate was the situation of the patricians. By the single word *veto*, "I forbid it," the tribune could hold any measure in suspense, and such a weapon was conceded only because something worse was feared.

The story of Coriolanus shows how bitter was the feeling in his order, and what a difficult task it must have been for the more moderate spirits to bring about a reconciliation through such sweeping concessions. Ship-loads of corn had been sent by a Greek city for the relief of the misery in Rome. When it was proposed in the Senate to distribute this among the suffering plebeians, the haughty patrician exclaimed, contemptuously, "Why do they ask for corn? They have got their tribunes. Let them go back to their Sacred Hill, and leave us to rule alone!" The tribunes sternly summoned Coriolanus to appear before them on account of this insolent language. He refused to appear, and then, enraged at finding he was not sustained by the body of the patricians, and shaking the dust of the ungrateful city from his feet, he went into voluntary exile, offered his services to the Volscians, the enemies of Rome, and returned at the head of an army. It is said that when his mother met him with bitter reproaches he relented, saying, "Oh! my mother, thou hast saved Rome, but lost thy son!" then returned to the Volscians to be slain for betraying their cause. The story is used by Shakespeare for one of his noblest dramas.

Although much had been gained there was still one deep-seated cause for poverty, which was reducing the most numerous body of Roman citizens to beggary. They had not land enough to feed them. A tract which in the time of the kings had been set apart as a royal domain, had, since the patricians returned to power, been used by them for pasturage. When Spurius Cassius, who was consul in 486 B.C., proposed an agrarian law, which should divide these public lands among the people, the patricians, as was natural, vehemently opposed it. But Cassius was determined and powerful, and the memory of the Sacred Hill was still fresh. It would be better to pass

the measure ... hey bided their
time. As so... a charge was
brought agai... said, was only
part of a wic... n making himself king. He ... demned to the
death of a tr... se razed to the
ground. The ... s, were always
agitators in t... entertainment
in forays und... nit outrages in
the plebeian ... crats was Kaeso Quinctius ... s. After some
particularly s... so, summoned
him to appea... was sent into exile.
When a band of Sabines, led by Roman exiles, a little later surprised the
city, many believed that the young Kaeso was one of the instigators. It was
soon after this that the Romans were defeated in a battle with the Volscians
and Equians, and their consul made a prisoner. The great Cincinnatus, father
of Kaeso, was appointed dictator, swiftly defeated the Volscians, made them
"pass under the yoke," released the consul, and then came back to. make the
tribunes feel the weight of his displeasure. No agrarian law, he declared,
should go into effect while he had power to prevent it. And probably no act
in his dictatorship pleased him more than inflicting condign punishment upon the accusers of his son Kaeso.

We strongly suspect that the old hero, when his triumphs were over, retired to his farm on the Campagna, not because he so loved democratic
simplicity, as that he so hated a rising democratic ascendancy, which was
dragging Rome down from her once high estate! They were degenerate days
indeed when low-born plebeians had power to arraign and punish patricians!
And we can imagine the tears of honest shame and humiliation shed by the
grand old aristocrat, whom we revere today as the supreme type of the democratic citizen.

Chapter VI

There was one powerful weapon held by the commons which no ingenuity of the patricians could take away from them. They could refuse to serve as soldiers; and this they were doing with increasing frequency; and when they did fight the spirit which had once made the legions invincible had departed. It was during the consulship of Kaeso Fabius that one of these crises arrived. The army, supported by the tribunes, refused to fight. The Fabian gens was one of the proudest among the patricians. They had led in the opposition to the agrarian law of Spurius Cassius, and also in his condemnation. It is not probable that the personal feelings of Fabius had changed, or that he felt any less bitterly than Coriolanus and Cincinnatus about the elevation of the commons. But he had the political wisdom to see the injury done to the state by withholding justice from the people whose services were indispensable to it. He suddenly changed his whole attitude, and threw the great weight of his name and influence into the advocacy of the cause he had tried to defeat. He insisted that the agrarian law should at once become operative; and when his arguments were treated with scorn by the patricians, the entire Fabian gens, numbering over three hundred, with their clients and their slaves, and a few patrician families who wished to share their fortunes, marched solemnly out of the city gates. Then, as if to emphasize the nobility of their purpose, they made a fortified camp on the borders of Etruria for the protection of Rome; and after doing the state good service for one year, were surprised during a religious festival by a band of Veintines and slaughtered to a man. The plebeians had lost their most powerful friends. The law of debt was unchanged. The enormous rate of interest had been reduced, but the savage penalties were the same. Soldiers returning from long campaigns and finding their children crying for bread would make loans from the rich and then become their slaves. The tribunes were unceasing in trying to obtain redress for special cases of oppression, but the main struggle of each tribunate was for their agrarian rights, encouraging the people to refuse to respond to the levies for troops until justice was done. At a time of extreme pressure the patrician lords made a concession; they granted the plebeians the Aventine Hill for their own possession (under the Icilian Law, which had long been urged). The land being insufficient to give one plot to each, several persons received one allotment, who jointly built their house, each story being occupied by a family. Such a residence being called *insulae* while *domus* is the term for the mansion occupied by a single family. But such concession gave only temporary relief and the relations of the orders were becoming more and more embittered. Appius Claudius, when his soldiers at a critical time refused to take the field against the Volscians, sternly commanded that every tenth man in his legions be put to death; and it was done. Then, when his consulship expired the proud Appius was summoned to appear before the tribunes, and realizing the humiliation and condemnation which awaited him he committed suicide.

It was a time full of peril for Rome. One tribune had been assassinated and also many leading plebeians, and there is a fearful story of eight tribunes being burned alive. Violence had taken the place of law, and unless the moderate spirits in both orders could check the rising tide of passion, civil war was inevitable. A truce was declared while some compromise could be considered. It was finally agreed that the existing troubles arose from the indefiniteness of the laws controlling the relations of the two orders. It was also agreed that a commission of ten should be appointed to draw up a legal code by which equal justice should be dealt out to the entire Roman people—patricians and plebeians alike. It was especially intended that this code should accurately determine the limits of authority to be exercised by magistrates, and the modes of redress and procedure in the protection of lives and property (the Terentillian Law). During these labors the patricians and the plebeians were to give up their consuls and their tribunes, and be entirely subject to the Council of Ten—which was to be chosen from both orders, and to be called "The Decemvirate" (450 B.C.).

Chief among these decemvirs was Appius Claudius, son of the consul of that name who executed every tenth man in his legion.

The Code of Laws which was the work of the first decemvirate is known as the "Twelve Tables," and it is now the basis of the legal systems of a large part of Europe, and of America. It was in the second decemvirate that the mask was thrown aside. Appius had made himself so popular that he was re-elected, and Rome soon found herself in the hands of a despot, with nine imitators ready to do his bidding. It was said that instead of one Tarquin, she now had ten. She seemed under a spell which she knew not how to break; and many citizens fled and joined the colonists outside.

There was living on the Aventine a wealthy plebeian named Virginius, a centurion. His daughter Virginia, as beautiful as the day, was betrothed to Icilius, a former tribune. Appius one morning chanced to see the young maiden on her way to school. He quickly ordered Claudius, one of his clients, to seize her and claim her as his slave. When her cries and those of her nurse attracted a crowd, Claudius explained that this girl was the child of his slave, and when an infant was stolen to fill the place of a child who had died in the house of Virginius. This he could prove. But he would lay his case before the Decemvir Appius and abide by his decision. The next morning Virginius and weeping friends were at the Forum when the child was brought before the great Appius; and when he gave judgment that she should remain in the custody of Claudius until Virginius had proved his right to her, they knew she was lost. The lictor advanced to seize her, Virginia humbly asked if he might speak one word with her before she was removed. Then taking her in his arms and whispering "It is the only way, my daughter," he plunged a knife into her bosom.

The whole of the Roman populace was aroused to a state of fury. The Senate called upon the decemvirs to resign. The commons without their tribunes were utterly defenceless, and knew not what fresh tyranny awaited them. Once more they marched to the Sacred Hill, there to treat with the ambassadors from the Senate, or there to remain, if their terms were not accepted.

They demanded three things: That their tribunes be restored; that the right of appeal from the sentence of the consuls be enjoyed by them as by the patricians; and that the ten decemvirs be burnt alive.

The last savage demand was abandoned, but the others were accepted by the Senate. The first act of the new tribunate, which now held ten tribunes, was the impeachment of Appius by Virginius, the charge being a violation of his own law, just framed in the Twelve Tables: "that a person claimed as slave, should be free until the claim was established." The proud patrician could not bear the humiliation of his downfall and, as his father had done not long before, committed suicide in prison.

As Lucretia had destroyed the monarchy, so the fair Roman child Virginia had overthrown the decemvirate.

There could be no settled peace until complete equality, social and political, was accorded to the commons. Another agitation quickly followed. Two laws were simultaneously proposed by the tribunes. The first of these was the Canuleian Law: legalizing marriage between the two orders. "If we are different races of men," said they, "if our blood will not mingle, then let us live apart." It was the old threat of secession; and after a storm of opposition the patricians yielded and the wall of caste was broken down. But the other demand attacked the last stronghold of patrician Rome, and eighty years were to pass before it would be conceded. It was that the consulship should be thrown open to plebeians. To refuse might be dangerous. The tribunes were reminded of the sacred duties belonging to the office, and that the auspices could only be taken by those in whose veins coursed pure patrician blood. And here again was the claim of a difference in kind, and another reason why, as the commons said, they should be a separate people.

Finally, a compromise was reached. Instead of a consulate there should, during a portion of the time, be a military tribunate, to which both orders were alike eligible. This was agreed to in 444 b.c., and not until 400 did a single plebeian fill the office! It was by such empty promises as this that the patient plebeians were again and again beguiled; a thing difficult to reconcile with that good faith which is the corner-stone of Roman character, the keystone of their arch. The Roman commons were not contending with an honorable foe, but a foe which under great pressure, would yield the point in dispute, and then by legislation deprive the thing granted of its value, or the office conceded of the authority it had hitherto possessed, and render the triumph void. The history of the long conflict is a succession of such tricks and evasions. Their honor and good faith consisted in fidelity to a code, not to a sense of right and justice; and their code did not recognize the plebeians as equals, hence promises to them had no binding power.

Chapter VII

Rome was now mistress of all of Latium. The Equians and Volscians had also been driven back by the renewed spirit in the legions and there had commenced a life and death struggle with the great Etrurian city of Veii. There was an old prediction that Veii would fall when the Alban Lake flowed into the sea—which meant—never. So although the city was besieged they were not dismayed. Then by orders of the Roman Senate, a tunnel was commenced leading from the lake to the river Anio. For a distance of three miles it was cut through volcanic stone, making an outlet five feet high and three feet wide; and the waters of the Alban Lake were soon flowing to the sea, and are doing so still! At the same time the great Caligula was digging a mine which terminated under the sanctuary in the citadel of the doomed city; and when armed Roman soldiers rose from the floor the prediction was fulfilled and Veii, like ancient Troy, had fallen. The city was thrown open to Roman colonists to the great relief of the plebeian quarter, and to the Veintines were assigned homes on the Caelian hill.

A new and unprecedented storm was about to break upon the Eternal City. The Gauls, those barbarians of Western Europe, who had long been troubling Etruria, were investing Clusium. That city appealed to Rome for help, and in response three envoys from the Senate met Brennus, the barbarian leader, and announced to him that Clusium was under Roman protection. But, they did something more than negotiate; they fought and rendered efficient service to their Etruscan friends in a battle which was in progress. Brennus was not so much of a barbarian that he did not understand his rights. He declared that the law of nations had been violated, and he should take immediate vengeance upon Rome. When the Romans learned that the Gauls were almost at their gates, there was a panic. They fled by thousands to Veii and other neighboring cities. Eighty venerable senators and a small force upon the rocky pinnacle of the capital alone remained. The Gauls, through open gates, entered a silent city, and when they reached the Forum they were awe-stricken. There sat eighty senators in their ivory chairs, venerable, silent, immovable. They believed a company of gods had come down from Heaven. But when one old man fiercely resented a touch upon his beard by a blow with his ivory staff, the spell was broken; he was slain, and then the rest were quickly dispatched. While the city was burning, and for months afterward, the Capitol on its rocky eminence was held by Manlius and his little band; every attempt to scale the slippery height being defeated; until that famous dawn when the geese gave warning that the enemy was coming; and the defenders had just time to hurl down those in advance who carried the rest with them. And so for seven months the Gauls rioted and waited, until at last, sated and demoralized, and with news of the invasion of their own homes in the North, they withdrew. Rome was only a blackened ruin. With, difficulty were the people dissuaded from abandoning it, and making Veil their city. But at last all had returned and were striving to re-build and efface the ravages of the destroying host. Again were the plebeians plunged in hopeless debt to the superior order; and again were all the rigors of the law of debt carried out without mercy. Manlius, upon see-ing some of his bravest soldiers, the defenders of the Capitol, dragged to prison, himself paid their debts. So frequently did he do this, and so bitterly did he reproach the patricians, that in exasperation they accused him of seeking popularity with ambitious designs. It was declared that his generosi-ty was only a part of a treasonable plot to make himself king. He was tried, condemned, and thrown off the Tarpeian rock— the rock which his valor had held for seven months, the one spot in Rome he had kept untouched by barbarian feet. The old conflict between the orders was reaching its final stage. Three laws were proposed by the Tribune Licinius; one mitigating the law of debt; another restricting the amount of land to be used by any indi-vidual; and the third that henceforth there be, not military tribunes, but two consuls; one of whom should always be a plebeian. These are known as the Licinian Rogations.

It was the iron will and the inflexible purpose of two tribunes, Caius Licinius and Lucius Sextius which accomplished the seemingly impossible task of compelling the patricians to yield to these demands. For ten years they labored, being reappointed nine times, and during all of the last five years using their right of veto to stop the wheels of government; not permit-ting a single levy for the army, nor the election of a single magistrate, consul, military tribune, questor, or censor. The Senate in despair called Camillus to The dictatorship. But when that wise old warrior saw the invin-cible spirit of the tribunes, he advised honorable capitulation. The patricians yielded. The long struggle was ended; and in 307 BC, the first plebeian con-sul, Lucius Sextus, took his place in the curule chair. Camilius vowed a temple to Concord in commemoration of the great event. He had won his laurel wreath at the capture of Veii. But as he who rules his spirit is greater than he who takes a city, so the brave Roman's chief title to glory is as "Ca-millus the Peace-Maker."

There was the usual attempt to impoverish the office by assigning its judicial functions to a praetor, an office then created for that purpose. But this was only delaying the inevitable; for in 351 b.c. the censorship was open to the commons; in 337 the praetorship was obtained; and in 300, plebeians filled the priestly offices of pontifex and augur, and by the year 172 B.C. the patrician families had so decreased that both consulships were held by plebeians. Political power had not been the aim, but by slow and painful steps it had been attained. With surprising moderation there had never been a single demand except for relief from specific grievances, touching persons and property.

The equalization of her commons and patricians is the central nerve in the history of the Republic. Her far-reaching conquests were a magnificent display of power. But it was the core of character created in the long internal struggle, which made that power possible, and which was the source of the enduring mastery of the empire, even after that character had long departed. Neither order could have made Rome. Each needed the other. The commons lacked the dignity and sense of mastery which comes from long established supremacy; and the patricians, debauched by the use and abuse of supreme power, must have perished without the infusion of fresh uncorrupted strength—the strength which comes from suffering patiently borne in a long, brave battle with oppression. This had been for the commons a political education and a training in the principle of justice. With strength no longer wasted at home, and with legions fighting as they had never fought before, an age of conquest began. There were some defeats (a colossal and bitter one at Candium, 321), but more victories, and, one by one, rival and hostile cities were being gathered into Roman dominion.

Chapter VIII

These were obscure events in those stirring times. The healing of a family quarrel at Rome was not discussed by the gay young revellers at Syracuse and Tarentum. There were great actors on the stage then, and momentous issues. The everlasting drama was being played. There were great powers, and lesser powers, and crumbling cities and nations that were no powers at all; and there was greed—greed for territory, and for mastery; and suspicion and fear, and craft, and cunning, all—all were there, while the struggle was going on for the grand prize, that dream of every ambitious nation—universal dominion. Sometimes Carthage and sometimes Greece was in the lead for this mastery in the Mediterranean world. Etruria, once powerful on the great stage, had lapsed into obscurity. Phoenicia, in utter decadence, was making futile attempts at self-preservation; Egypt, Persia, and even Assyria and Chaldea, in their own decrepitude, making her last days miserable. Greece and Carthage, in the plenitude of their strength, were the two gladiators. Mutually antagonistic, one stood for the supreme type of civilization, the other for the incarnation of the spirit of trade without one humanizing trait; the wicked child of an even more wicked Asiatic mother. No greater misfortune could come to the world than for Carthage to obtain the mastery; and that was what many times seemed imminent, as she battered away at the beautiful old Greek cities which studded the shores of Southern Italy and of Sicily. It was these incessant conflicts, and the fatal rivalries among themselves which had reduced the splendid constellation of Greek colonies to a few flickering stars, Sybaris, Paestum, Cumae, already in ruins. Wherever Greek civilization came, there came also the life-giving principle; and where the cruel grasp of Carthage fastened, there was arrested life and hopeless sodden barbarism; as illustrated by Sicily, the most brilliant spot in the pre-Roman world, and Sardinia and Corsica her Carthaginian sisters, the drudges and slaves of a cruel mistress. Such were the conditions, and such the actors in the pre-Roman drama; and when one of those periodical storms swept over the Mediterranean, the feeble clutched tighter their precarious kingdoms, and the Russias and the Englands watched eagerly to see how they might emerge from the chaos, richer and greater than before; the feeble watching how they too might pick up a few crumbs wherewith to renew their failing strength.

But Greece, with a fatal political system, wise in all wisdom except political wisdom, could never have attained universal dominion. Joined to her tremendous power of will, Rome had an instinct for organization. Now, with her fresh accession of military strength, with a perfect and willing instrument at hand to carry out the mandates of her imperious will, and with a renewed and consolidated organism to embody her administrative genius, the City of the Seven Hills was unconsciously moving toward that universal mastery of which she had never dreamed. The mastery even over her own peninsula was unpremeditated; like England in India, each advance made to protect those already made, and for the preservation of the whole. So not by her own seeking she was approaching the frontiers of the great arena.

In the study of history nothing is more obvious than the unconsciousness with which men and nations and empire, intent only upon their own selfish purposes, are developing vast designs of which they have never thought. Rome's advent upon the great stage was at the right moment. It would have been futile before the recent crisis in her internal life; and for the nascent Roman power to have been overthrown by Carthage or by Alexander, as it might have been had he lived, would have removed the foundations of civilization as it exists today. So persistently does this thread of divine purpose run through history, ancient and modern, working out the predetermined plan, the inference becomes irresistible that the overturnings of nations for selfish and temporary ends are only stitches in a design so vast it must be seen through the perspective of years, or of centuries. Aided by the Gauls, all of Italy was finally aroused to a combined effort at self-preservation. It was a terrible school for the legions, they were being welded into men of steel. Nothing could stand before them. One by one the Northern nations succumbed, and when the powerful Samnites in the South were vanquished, all of Italy had become Roman (272 B.C.).

But if the Roman legions had vanquished the Italian States, it was the administrative genius of Rome which retained them in her tenacious grasp. By converting Volscians, Etruscans, Samnites, at once into Romans— by establishing in the conquered provinces a vital and intimate relation with Rome, and Rome alone—by entangling them in the meshes of an ingeniously woven net of sovereignty from which they could not escape— once hers, she made them hers forever. The difference between Greek and Roman colonization was characteristic. The Greek colony became an independent organism; the Roman, only an extension of the metropolis. Each city was only a smaller Rome, with its patricians, its Senate, its two chief magistrates—and a system of carefully restricted Roman citizenship. Perfectly unique in its conception, this was the nucleus of a vast empire governed by a single city.

In weaving this magnificent system over the peninsula, Rome was unconscious of its wisdom, and that it would serve when her provinces extended from the British Isles to Chaldea. The Roman brain was a very simple affair beside that of the Greek. It had no subtleties; was not brilliant nor speculative. Their government was not the result of theory, but of experiment, always moving with a sure instinct toward that which made for power and permanence in institutional life. There was not a man in the Senate who could have discussed the theory of government with the philosophic Greeks; but by intuition they had discovered what the Greeks would have done well to learn—the power of the associative principle.

But the collective incapacity of the Greeks was precisely due to their transcendent individual greatness. It would be difficult to say whether the world could better have spared Greece or Rome. Both were building empires indispensable and imperishable.

By the year 480, the invading Persian hosts had been driven by the Greek States back into Asia. Then Athens had her peerless day under Pericles and her brief age of supremacy, to be quickly extinguished by the deadly conflict with envious Sparta—the Peloponnesian War—when Greek met Greek, and for thirty-seven years the peninsula was rent and torn, and finally, when Athens had surrendered, when her beauty had been defaced and trampled upon by scoffing Spartans, the old Greece had departed.

Her interior life was gone. In 338 the enfeebled disorganized States found a master. Out of rough untutored Macedon came Philip, and gathered the struggling incohesive mass into his own strong keeping. In vain did Demosthenes utter his impassioned philippics. In vain did he appeal to pride of race and patriotism. The patriotism and the vigor of the Senate had been sapped. Greece was helpless in the grasp of the Macedonian. Then came Philip's assassination, and a brief dream of escape when his son Alexander, a beardless youth of only twenty, succeeded him (336). But in two more years this boy, with the face and form of a god, had riveted the chains tighter than before, and was sweeping across into Asia to vanquish the Persians. This done, Tyre, then Gaza fell before him, and the invincible youth, after pausing in Egypt and founding his city, swept on, conquering and capturing from the Caspian to the Indies, planting Greek colonies and thickly strewing the seeds of Hellenic civilization by the way; and after only ten years, was sitting at Babylon, holding his court in Oriental splendor, receiving embassies and the homage due to a divinity.

Among these embassies it is said there was one from the Samnites praying for aid in driving back the Romans, that hitherto obscure people, who were absorbing the Italian peninsula, and becoming a menace to the old Greek cities by the sea. Had this invincible man lived to return, the course of history must have been changed. His insatiable ambition was already planning an extension of his empire westward. Italy and Sicily would have been swallowed up by the way, and Alexander not Rome would have performed the task of overthrowing the Carthaginian Empire. But this was not to be. In 232, Alexander succumbed to fever, and died at Babylon, the capital of a colossal empire which was destined to fall into pieces when his mighty hand was withdrawn.

The ancient Greek city of Tarentum, heretofore protected by the warlike Samnites, now saw herself on the borders of that new barbaric power with its home upon the Tiber. Helpless, luxurious, living upon the traditions of former greatness, the proud city soon came into collision with Rome. The Roman Senate was weary of war. But when their ambassador arrived in Tarentum to negotiate a peace, the gay young Tarentines, who were in the midst of a wild religious festival, received his bad Greek with shouts of derisive laughter. It was an ill-timed insult. War was declared, and Tarentum appealed to Pyrrhus, young king of Epirus, to undertake her defence. Full of the spirit of adventure, and with ambitious dreams of his own, Pyrrhus gladly responded, and for the first time the Roman legion met the Greek phalanx. Unused to the different mode of warfare, and demoralized by the elephants, the defeat of the Romans was inevitable. But Pyrrhus exclaimed, "One more such victory, and I am undone!" and again—"Had I such soldiers, the world would be mine!" The Greek Cineas, whom he sent to treat with the Senate, returning, said: "To fight these people is like fighting the Hydra!" Amazed at what he saw at Rome, he exclaimed, "Their city is a temple, and their Senate an assembly of kings!" So, after many costly and barren victories, this romantic, chivalrous young king, who so resembles Charles XII of Sweden in character and in career, abandoned the Italian peninsula and his dream of playing Alexander in the West (278 B.O.).

Rome was being gradually drawn toward the vortex of the political whirlpool in the south, the centre of which vortex had always been Sicily. Partly Carthaginian and partly Greek, this island had been for centuries the storm centre; the brilliant city of Syracuse, many times laid low by its Carthaginian neighbor, Agrigentum, and many times rising again from its ashes more splendid than before.

It was in 264 BC that Rome passed the dividing line between obscurity and greatness, and entered the great arena by way of an insignificant door which opened to her in Sicily. No less heroic, or even less reputable cause was ever championed, or ever ushered in a train of events so tremendous. A marauding band of mercenaries from Campania, called Mammertines, had taken possession of the little town of Messana in Sicily, had murdered the males, and then appropriated their homes and wives and daughters. When the Syracusans attempted to dislodge this community of pirates, the Mammertines appealed to Rome for protection. The Senate was not in favor of espousing such a cause. It was a disreputable one, and would also be a challenge to either Greeks or Carthaginians.

But the Roman people had acquired an insatiate appetite for military conquests, and the protection asked for was voted by the popular assembly. Thus was commenced that series of wars which were to extend over a period of 118 years; and as the Phoenician language spoken by the Carthaginians was called by the Romans Punic, these are known as the Punic Wars.

Carthage, with her wealth and her power was a prodigious engine of cruelty. She ruled her colonies with excessive rigor, imposing tribute that it required all their industry to pay. The government was an oligarchy. A few aristocratic families descended from Tyrian kings held the power of the state, which was chiefly vested in a council of one hundred, elected by themselves for life. The military generals, selected not because of fitness, but on account of personal relations with the heads of the oligarchy, if unsuccessful, were beheaded or crucified by their aristocratic friends. As this latter was their favorite mode of punishment, it seems not improbable that crucifixion came into Rome by way of Carthage. With such a nation Rome had embarked upon a struggle which would survive four generations of men.

Herself a novice upon the sea, she had challenged the greatest maritime power then existing. It was an untried path, which only a strange indwelling consciousness of power could have ventured upon. There were many defeats. But there was somewhat in these Romans which made them rise stronger from defeat than their enemies from victory. Their fleet might be stranded on the African coast, its commander, Regulus, a prisoner. But the man who could bring back to his city offers of peace from his captors— advise that they be not accepted—and then return to certain death by torture, reveals a source of strength which cannot be measured. Whether true or legendary, this story explains the miracle of Rome's invincibility. When the first Punic War was finished Sicily was a Roman province; humiliating terms had been imposed upon Carthage. Hanno, her unfortunate general, had been crucified, and the great Hamilcar, with Spain as his military basis, was planning to recover Sicily, and Sardinia and Corsica which had also been ceded, his boy, Hannibal, in camp with him, in training for his own part in the struggle.

It was when this boy succeeded to the command in Spain that the conflict began to assume its colossal dimensions. The ancient Greek city of Saguntum, which for centuries had looked out upon the sea, was in alliance with Rome. Her destruction was the first note of defiance. Hannibal then proceeded to realize his stupendous plan. The Romans had carried the war into Africa, now he would carry it into Italy. He would march through Gaul, across the Alps, there reinforced by the Cisalpine Gauls—those tireless tormentors of Rome—what matter if half his men perished by the way!—and on the plains of Italy he would be met by Hasdrubal his brother, with another great Carthaginian army, and Rome would be theirs. This gigantic plan, as great in execution as in conception, met its final climax at Cannae (216). The Consul Fabius who, by long and skilfully evading a conflict, gave his name to that policy of delay, was replaced by the impetuous Varro, and the battle was fought—and lost. Forty thousand Romans were lying dead upon the field, and an easy path seemed open to Rome. Varro was not crucified, but commended by the undaunted Roman Senate for his faith in the Republic, while with lofty courage it levied boys, slaves, anyone who could carry arms, to fill up the fresh legions. In this hour of Carthaginian ascendancy, while the fate of the Republic was trembling in the balance, the lifeless Greek States, like driftwood, were swept into the swiftest current. Macedonia made alliance with Hannibal. This sealed the fate of Greece. The invading army of Hannibal was soon acting on the defensive. The great Scipio had driven the last Carthaginian out of Spain, and was in Africa. By the year 183 B.C. Hannibal was a fugitive and a suicide. In 171 the king of Macedonia was adorning a triumphal procession in the streets of Rome—and by the year 146 every Greek state had been subjugated. Carthage, as a city or even as a name, no longer existed, but was known as the Roman province of Africa.

Chapter IX

Rome, the heart and centre of this great expansion, so wise in all that made for conquest and power and authority, failed to recognize that simple truth which great nations today are so slow to learn—that in order to be really sound a nation must be sound in all its parts; that for its common people to be in abject misery while a favored class is enjoying the fruits of its increased prosperity, is to bear the seeds of dissolution within itself. Every year the gulf had been growing wider between the two classes—no longer patrician and plebeian—but the aristocratic class and the people. As the thirst for wealth and political ascendancy grew in the one, the sense of injustice deepened in the other. Appius Claudius, he who built the Appian Way and who was consul during the war with Pyrrhus, cunningly strove to offset the majorities of the common people by bestowing the franchise upon the freedmen, the children of emancipated slaves, who were the natural adherents of his order; at the same time striving to win the support of the commons by bringing to the thirsty Aventine the first great aqueduct. But much as they needed water, the dwellers outside the sacred city limits needed land more; and the entire disregard of the Licinian Law, restricting the amount of public domain to be used by one person, was engendering destructive forces which threatened more disaster to the Republic than had Carthaginians or Macedonians. The vast wealth which poured into Rome after the conquest of these nations passed into the hands of a few, and these few, by still further extending the franchise to strangers, also continued to keep in their own hands the administration of the affairs of the Republic. They alone were reaping the benefit from the enormous sacrifices borne alike by all for generations. Thousands of Roman citizens, men who were soldiers and patriots, had become beggars and vagrants, and the wise, even among the nobles, realized that the Republic was falling into an abyss from which they might be powerless to extricate it. A crisis was inevitable. It came in 133, when the Tribune Tiberius Sempronius Gracchus attempted to re-enact the Licinian Law. In the riots which ensued, Gracchus, with many of his followers, was slain, and the work of reform was taken up by his younger brother, Caius Sempronius Gracchus. The destructive forces underlying the whole social condition had begun to escape, and a revolution had commenced which was to terminate only with the Republic, and with the advent of the great master—Julius Caesar.

Rome had passed her splendid climacteric when in native simplicity and with phenomenal strength she burst the bonds of her barbaric chrysalis and declared herself mistress of the Mediterranean, and when by sheer force of ability and of character she compelled the ancient world to bow down before her, and to wear the yoke she herself had so skilfully forged. But when she became debauched, with power and wealth, when avarice and greed had corrupted her heart, and when undigested foreign refinements and learning had corrupted her morals, the descent was swift. If ever she had need to be strong and wise it was when that torrent from the Orient and from Greece and from Africa was submerging the Roman nation. The nobility for which the word Roman stands belongs to the period of her isolation. When the Roman Senate, the greatest representative body that ever existed, with unexampled wisdom and dignity was guiding the State and keeping sacred its honor, and when noble Romans vied with each other in sacrifices for the Republic. But a different casuality was expressed by the name now, when a despicable aristocracy was revelling in coarse splendor and sensuous luxury, and famishing multitudes were willing to exchange their manhood and their votes for corn and gladiatorial shows; and when all alike were becoming brutalized by the passion for Roman combats, which popular sentiment demanded must be fought to the death. Still there were some who realized the degradation which had come upon the ancient city, and as Lucullus stands for the lavish splendor of this age, so Cato no doubt represents the sentiment of many in clinging to the austere simplicity of the Republic in its best days.

Imbeddled in the mass of avarice and crime and cruelty and of unassimilated foreign elements, we find the Jugurthine War. Called to defend the people of Numidia from Jugurtha, a criminal usurper, the Roman leaders, corrupted by bribes, were conniving at his crimes. No such disgrace had ever come upon Roman arms. Metellus, who did what he could to efface the stain, brought Jugurtha to Rome, where he perished, it is said, by starvation. But out of this Jugorthine infamy came Marius, the great leader of the popular party. Humble in origin, and with an ability which matched his ambition, he succeeded Metellus in the command of the army in the East; then, burning with hatred of the aristocratic party, he organized the revolutionary forces and led them against the party of oppression under Sulla in a civil war, a war in which rivers of blood flowed in vain, and in which the Republic virtually perished. When the victorious Sulla in 82 was proclaimed dictator for an indefinite period, the Republic was dead.

The machinery of government might go on from the old momentum and wars be fought, but the life of the organism was extinct; and the mass of heterogeneous elements was waiting to become the prey of the ablest among the men to be seen about the Forum. Would this be Pompey, the successful general who brought to a close the war with Mithridates, King of Pontus, and then distributed thrones in Syria, as if already a king, wearing the while such a pleasant cloak of humility. It was a game in politics the most desperate the world ever saw, and the most tremendous in results; a game in which every player wore a mask, and with consummate art was seeking the thing he pretended not to want. The prizes wore the grand old names, consul, quaestor, praetor, censor, pontifex maximus; but these were only points of vantage by which to seize the real thing—the reins of power in the perishing Republic. Foremost in this group at the Forum are Pompey, Crassus, Cicero, Catiline, Clodius and Caesar. Pompey was far in advance of the others, until Cicero, by unmasking and defending Catiline's deep-laid conspiracy, proclaimed himself the saviour of his country. The plan of that young patrician profligate was to extricate himself from a load of debt by setting fire to the city of Rome, overthrowing the Constitution, and then, in the general confusion, seizing the reins of government. A large number of reckless young aristocrats were drawn by him into the plot, which was unmasked by Cicero. But if this made the great orator popular with the people, it had a contrary effect with a great part of the patricians, more or less involved in the infamy.

Yet the men engaged in the game for power did not know that they were playing with a master, a man supremely great In everything he undertook. Not more pure than they in his motives, not more scrupulous in his methods, Caius Julius Caesar was yet the one man living who had the ability to lift Rome out of the abyss into which she had fallen.

Never was the golden thread of divine purpose more obvious than in placing this prodigy among men at that gateway between the past and the future ; behind him the ages of conflict with the powers of darkness, before him the kingdom of the Prince of Peace and of love and of light! Since the founding of Rome the trend had been steadily toward this climax. Rome could not perish, for her work had only just commenced—a work for which the ages behind her had been merely a preparation; this was, to gather up and to conserve the priceless riches of Greek culture and thought, and then to receive and to hold that other life-creating stream which was about to come into the world. Greek civilization and Christianity were the mind and soul of the coming race of man; and these, it was the appointed task of Rome to hold as in a reservoir, and then to open up channels for their distribution to the nations of the earth. Caesar's was the mighty hand chosen to convert the perishing Roman Republic into a suitable instrument for this task, to gather up its latent energies stored in the days of the old republic, to consolidate and to reconstruct all of its inchoate elements into an empire. It would need force of an appalling nature to accomplish what this empire would have to do. In that pre-Christian world love was not an active force.

The empire was to be cruel, pitiless, awe-inspiring, adamantine and impregnable, for it must endure for four centuries, and would have need of all its vast riches and resources in order to accomplish its appointed task. But it would be done, and the five short years of Caesar's sovereignty would contain the germs of a future Europe, and of the world's development as it exists today.

But at the time we have reached, Caesar was only one of many aspirants for leadership. He was a patrician among patricians, for did he not belong to the great Julian gens, descended from gods and kings! But what he kept most prominently before the people was his connection with the rough soldier Marius; their adored leader, whose nephew he was by marriage, but whose name must not be whispered now, in this age of aristocratic supremacy. So, by fearlessly, audaciously, associating himself with the popular cause, by skilfully ingratiating himself always with the people, he rose step by step until he was consul; the very first act being the passing of an agrarian law which bestowed vast tracts of public lands in Campania and other provinces, thus relieving the congested misery which was seven stories deep in the insular upon the Aventine. Then followed his amazing military successes until the final conquest of Gaul. Pompey saw his own victories in the east eclipsed by those of Caesar in the west, and his long ascendency slipping into the hands of his rival. There was only one thing to be done: that I was to disarm him. Not long before this, Pompey and Caesar and Crassus had formed a friendly alliance (the first Triumvirate) to curb a growing oligarchy in the Senate. But in the swiftly changing scene, Pompey was now in high favor and in close alliance with this senatorial power, and at his instigation the order was given for Caesar to disband his army: Cato, standing ready the moment he arrived in Rome to accuse him, and to bring about his impeachment.

All of Rome was now ready to prostrate itself at the feet of the conqueror; and the streets of that city had never beheld anything like the triumph awarded him. Gauls, Egyptians, Asiatics, Africans in chains, represented the list of his conquests; the most significant of all, that of Pompey, conspicuous in its absence! A frantic joy took possession of the whole people. The Senate, abject in flattery, named after him the month in which he was born—Julius—or July. They laid at his feet every power, every title, and dictatorship for life. He asked only to be consul; but while wearing this modest title he was in fact sovereign of a Roman Empire and of the world. The adulation of a god he received as if it were only his due, but as if it wearied him. Vast plans of reconstruction filled his mind; the Empire no longer to be ruled by a single city—Rome, its capital, not mistress. He was awakening dead patriotism, and opening channels by which it might give life and warmth to the remotest parts of the organism; reforming the calendar; adapting the ancient code of laws to new conditions. A man of the future, he was standing amid the wreck of the traditions of the past, and the world will never cease to wonder what might have been the outcome, had a complete system, bearing the stamp of his genius, been allowed to mature. Fragmentary and incomplete as it was, it changed the whole direction of human events. But a revulsion of feeling was setting in. This clemency to the people was suspicions, and this opening of the franchise to his Gauls, and the Senate to foreign people, seemed all a part of some gigantic plan of enslavement. To be adored by the people had always been reason enough for the destruction of a leader. A few jealous senators and a small number of men influenced, some by personal spite, and some by the madness which makes of tyrannicide a sacred duty, formed a plan for his assassination. Brutus, "Caesar's angel," as Shakespeare calls him, was reminded that his great progenitor delivered them from the Tarquins, did not receive favors from them! Of all the blows which rained upon him that 15th of March, "when the great Cippar fell" at the foot of Pompey' s statue, it was that of Brutus which pained him most; for "then his great heart broke," and he covered his head with his mantle, and accepted his fate.

They had thought to kill him, but Caesar dead was more powerful than Caesar living. Another revulsion set in. His generosity, his magnanimity were recalled; and when Mark Antony in his funeral oration, recited his gifts to the people, and showed the wounds inflicted by the "envious Casca," and by Cassius, it was received with a passion of grief; and when he read Caesar's will, bequeathing rich provinces to his murderers, one to Cassius, another to Casca, and to Brutus Cisalpine Gaul and the guardianship of his nephew and heir, Octavius, then the people were wrought to such a state of fury that the assassins had to flee from the city.

Chapter X

Rome was now without a master. Out of the chaos there came a Second Triumvirate, composed of Octavius, Antony, and Lepidus, who divided the world between them; Antony the East, Octavius the West, and Lepidus Africa. The enemy of one, was to be the enemy of all. So Cicero, who had been striving by his philippics to destroy Antony, was among the multitude of the proscribed, and was slain in his garden. Brutus and Cassius pursued by Antony, perished at Philippi, and met their victim and their Judge. But it was in Egypt that Antony had met his fate, when he became ensnared by that Circe of the Nile, Cleopatra. So infatuated did the once great tribune and general become, that he divorced his wife, the sister of Octavius; and when the Senate learned that the great Triumvir was bestowing Roman territory upon the children of Cleopatra, he was deprived of his powers, and Octavius sailed for the East with a fleet. The defeat at Actium (31 B.C.) made of Egypt a Roman province, and was quickly followed by the suicide of the disgraced Antony; and then by that of Cleopatra, who rather than endure the fate of adorning the triumph of Octavius at Rome, destroyed herself. The Senate bestowed upon Octavius the name Augustus—the Illustrious, and the month in (which he had won Egypt) was called after him - August. The other triumvir, Lepidus, was soon effaced, and Augustus Caesar was undisputed master of the world.

Politics no longer offered a field for ambitious Romans, and their immense activities flowed into a new channel. Since the Macedonian conquests had flooded Rome with Greek scholars, Hellenic learning and ideals had become a passion. Sitting at the feet of their slaves, men like Cicero had become not alone learned, but deeply imbued with Greek culture, and there had commenced a splendid imitation of Athenian thought. Without the creative genius of their great models, a literature came into being which makes the Augustan Age second only to that of Pericles. In the pause between the old and the new, in the tranquil interval between the passing of the Roman Republic and the coming of that supreme factor, Christianity, are found the names Lucretius, Virgil, Horace, Ovid, Strabo, to be soon followed by Pliny, Seneca, Plutarch, and Juvenal. The name of Caesar heads this illustrious group. Great in authorship as in all else, Caesar's Commentaries place him among the fathers of Roman literature in the pre-Augustan age.

This golden age in literature was a time of gilded splendor in all things. There was luxury, sensuous, gross, and barbaric in excess; enough to have made the austere Cato clothe himself in sackcloth if he had not already committed suicide over the fall of Pompey and of the republic. But the expanding thought and the triumphs in literature had given a deeper meaning and a richer coloring to life; and the distempers which attend imperialism had not yet developed. Their Caesar had not abused the opportunity created for him by the great Caesar, and Rome, content and triumphant, was the blazing centre of the world.

At this moment, in the small Roman province of Judea, and in Bethlehem, the most obscure town in Judea, there was born a child. There was no room for his mother at the inn, so the stable was his birthplace, and the manger his cradle. It would be thirty years before Rome would hear of this child Jesus, and then only as a harmless fanatic who had made himself offensive to the Jews. But in three centuries more, the waning Roman Empire would be trying to reinforce her strength and hide her decrepitude beneath his great mantle, and would acknowledge him King of Kings. And the glory of Rome would forever after be that it was the throne of his empire.

As the reign of Augustus was drawing to its close, and while he was weeping for his lost legions, lured by Hermann into the depths of the German forest and slain,—at this very time the boy Christ was in the temple at Jerusalem confounding the wisdom of the wise, while "his mother sought him sorrowing."

The period between Augustus and Vespasian, which reached its climax in Nero, is one of unmitigated and revolting atrocities. Men hitherto gentle and human in their impulses seem, at the touch of the imperial throne, to have been converted into monsters. Tiberius, the admirable soldier, who succeeded Augustus, quickly reached this transformation. In creating the Praetorian Guards, he converted the empire into a military despotism. This body of ten thousand men was an instrument of his own use, which at any moment might be employed against the people. The assemblies were abolished, their functions transferred to the Senate, which body was now reduced to a mere slavish instrument to wreak the personal vengeance of the emperor; its chief function being to try cases of high treason against his person. Spies and informers were lurking everywhere: death without trial inevitably following arrest. The furies seem to have been let loose in the land; a being of inconceivable cruelty on the throne, alternately resigning himself to debauchery, and to torturing fits of remorse; earthquakes, conflagrations, and disaster abroad;—it was in such a time of lurid horror that the Roman Governor Pilate, in the judgment hall at Jerusalem, was washing his hands of the responsibility he was about to assume, saying,—"I am innocent of the blood of this just person—see ye to it." Is it strange that the earth trembled, and that there was terror and despair, and that mercy and justice and hope seemed dead in the Roman Empire, while the Son of Man was being scourged and crucified. Upon the death of Tiberius, the Praetorian Guards, the Senate, and the people united in calling Caligula, the excellent son of a noble sire, to the throne. His father was Germanicus, the great general. For nearly a year he inspired confidence and hope. Then, seized by a sudden illness, the transformation came; arid on his recovery, he too was a monster. The excesses of his cruelties and of his vices, and his hunger for adulation, offset by nobility, made him an object of contempt as well as horror; and while insisting that he be worshipped as a god, he was cut down by his own Praetorian Guards; to be followed by Claudius, not vicious, but a weakling. The demons passing him by, seem to have entered into his two wives; first Messalina, whose atrocious profligacy is an explanation, if not a justification, of her execution by the order of Claudius her husband; who then immediately married the more able and no less vicious Agrippina, by whom he himself was assassinated in order to secure the throne for her son Nero; she to be in turn assassinated by this very son, when he had come well under the spell of madness which inevitably attended such elevation! Nero's reign was a climax, and it fittingly ushered in the persecution of that obscure Jewish sect—the Christians, whom Tacitus says had rendered themselves odious "by their hatred of the human race!" Rome was nearly destroyed by a conflagration. Nero was suspected of having kindled it, and in order to divert suspicion from himself, he charged it upon the Christians. Ingenious cruelties were devised for their death—it was an opportunity to amuse the people. They were covered with the skins of wild beasts and thrown into the arena, nailed to crosses, and at night were made human torches to illumine Nero's gardens. It was in the outburst of fury during this persecution that Peter and Paul are said to have perished in Rome. Like that of his predecessors, the death of Nero was a violent one and occurred in 68 a.d.

In viewing this horrible century after Julius Caesar one asks why his agency in human affairs should be exalted. But his work had been wrenched from his hand, fragmentary and incomplete. Caesar would never have degraded the Roman Senate and extinguished the voice of the people; not because he was beneficent, but because he was wise, his genius instinct with the spirit of the future. But the empire, rigid and inexorable with the strength he had infused into it, had fallen into the hands of madmen, and was to remain a soulless engine of power and cruelty for four centuries. With the reign of Vespasian better times came. The building of the Coliseum, and the fall of Jerusalem mark this period. Josephus, who was one of the Jewish captives taken in Galilee, has preserved for us the details of the great tragedy, when the city, besieged by Titus, son of Vespasian, finally fell; and when the people found their last refuge in the Temple, and perished with it (70 A.D.). It was during the succeeding reign of Titus that the eruption of Vesuvius occurred which destroyed the old Greek cities of Pompeii and Herculaneum (79 a.d.)., Roman power had now extended over Britain and Agricola was building his wall across the isthmus between England and Scotland. Trajan's was the most humane and enlightened reign which had yet come; a wise statesmanship striving to re-establish some of the ancient freedom; and Trajan's Column, erected by a grateful senate and people, stands today as his memorial. The reign of Marcus Aurelius, "a sage upon a throne" (161-180 A.D.), closed this benign period; and was a climax of excellence and virtue, as Nero's had been one of wickedness. A love of learning and a passion for morality joined to a singularly devout nature, made of this man a shining exemplar of the Stoic philosophy which so powerfully influenced Roman thought and life. But although truly intent upon the happiness and well-being of all created things, the illustrious pagan did not rebuke the frightful Christian persecutions, which after long cessation broke out afresh in his empire.

It is impossible to understand the mental attitude of educated Romans during this period without understanding Stoicism, that Greek exotic which so profoundly penetrated Roman life and institutions. The ancient mythology had long ago become assimilated with that of Greece. But while their gods were the same, the religion had for the Romans an essentially different character. It was for them a compact of mutual obligations between gods and men. In return for certain rites and observances, these beings, greater than themselves, were to bestow benefits here, and an immunity from suffering hereafter. It was a cool, passionless contract, equally binding upon both. Its once powerful hold had gradually weakened, and with the influx of Greek thought and the consequent awakening of Roman intelligence, augurs and auspices had become of small account, and the whole sacerdotal system an empty shell. But a reliance upon something outside of, and greater than ourselves, is a necessity for the human soul; and the Roman mind began to search among the things new and strange which had poured into Rome—the magic, the astrology, the Greek philosophies, the Egyptian and Oriental mysteries—for something to satisfy this hunger. In Stoicism they found a philosophy precisely suited to the native Roman character. It was noble and it was heroic. It was hard, unloving, but it was courageous and true. It justified the Roman to himself, and made of his moral deficiencies the loftiest virtue. They had never known mercy, nor pity, nor any tender emotion; so a philosophy which made the absence of these weaknesses its main tenet was congenial. Stoicism was a rigid ethical system under the guidance of human reason. It was an austere, uncompromising pursuit of virtue without hope of reward, here or hereafter. And this virtue must proceed from the will, not the emotions. Clemency was a virtue, but pity a weakness. Death, sickness, loss, were not evils, only opportunity for more virtue in despising their efforts to torment you. Anaxagoras on being told of the death of his son simply said; "I never supposed I had begotten an immortal." The fountain of benevolence, of tears for others' woes, would inevitably be dried by such a system. It was a moral monstrosity; but it had within it a regenerating principle, and a profound basic truth. Virtue in Rome, where all existed for the state, meant political virtue; and this meant an awakening of character, and the enormous power attained by Stoicism in that period of deepest corruption, from Cato to Marcus Aurelius, was a natural effort toward the rehabilitation of character; and is a proof of the inherent tendency toward moral health, still existing in the nation. It is the strangest of anomalies to see this stream of austere virtue threading its way through the mass of loathsome licentiousness, gathering up volume and strength and entering into the structure of Roman Institutions. It is found today imbedded in Roman jurisprudence. The principle underlying Stoic philosophy, and which was its life, was that of the universal brotherhood of humanity, a unity by virtue of a law of nature, knitting men into one body; and added to this a recognition of the inherent dignity of man, which circumstances could not impair or touch. These lay at the very basis of the question of human rights and of equity; and Roman law; as formulated by its great expounders in those days, in its language and in its spirit, bears the unmistakable impress of Stoicism.

But while profoundly true in its basic principles Stoicism was an unnatural, passionless system to live by. It was a deliberate attempt to eliminate the divine and the spontaneous, to dry up the springs of hope and love and pity and of joy. It is remembered only as one of the diseased phases of the human soul on its way toward peace; and it is a significant fact that Greece fed upon the dry husks of Stoicism in the days of her intellectual decline, and Rome in the period of her moral decay. It was a rugged staff which both used as a support in times of desperate need and indigence, and then threw away.

Understanding his philosophy, we can also understand why the gentle and devout Marcus Aurelius was not moved by the torturing of Christians at Lyons, and are not surprised that poets and writers who constantly lauded virtue and decried vice, found their recreation in witnessing the horrible sufferings in I the arena. Nor does it appear so inconceivable that in the reign of the excellent Titus, three thousand gladiators perished for the entertainment of Rome, and in that of the good and beneficent Trajan—ten thousand!

Epicureanism, which made pleasure, not virtue, its end, never attained such an influence. It was moving with the popular stream, so had not the power which attends a reaction. But both Greek Platonism and oriental mysticism strongly appealed to many minds. Platonism, which was monotheistic, included a belief in a system of spiritual daemons or divinities which were the agents of the divine will. It was this belief which linked it with oriental mysticism, which claimed that there was a divine indwelling which was the all-good, and which could be invited into the soul by austerities and meditation, inducing a state of spiritual exaltation. So these two blended into a Neo-Platonism which was destined to supersede Stoicism. Stoicism and Neo-Platonism were as wide apart as Ptolemaic and Copernican astronomy. Stoicism made man the active centre, Neo-Platonism made him the passive recipient from the divine centre.

Stoicism made human reason the sole guide, Neo-Platonism discarded the teachings of reason, and listened for the voice of the divine indwelling; silence and meditation its teachers. It was the same ancient wisdom as that now taught by men from the East, who doubtless walked the streets of Rome, olive-skinned, turbanned, serene in their orientalism, just as they do here today, expounding the philosophy of existence which was old before Rome or Aeneas or Troy existed.

Par down beneath this ferment of thought, and this turbid mingling of Roman depravity and eastern subtleties, there were flowing unseen rivulets of truth, the simplest ever presented to man; truths uttered in Galilee by Him who was scourged and crucified at Jerusalem. As Greek and Asiatic slaves had brought their system and taught them to their masters, so Judean slaves, especially since the fall of Jerusalem, had brought the story of the life and death of their Christ, for whom so many had already suffered and died during the early days of the empire. Pounded upon miraculous stories concerning a Nazarene carpenter, stories unsupported by evidence, is it strange that they heard nothing of this "still small voice," and heeded not if they heard? They were listening for the whirlwind. But the gentle teachings of the new religion, its pare and noble system of ethics—the compassion and love it offered from One who was Himself "a Man of Sorrows and acquainted with grief" and "touched with a feeling for our infirmities,"—all this sank deep into sin-sick hearts. The simplicity of the message, and the peace it brought was winning disciples— disciples who would spread the glad tidings, and in their rapture court death and beg the privilege of martyrdom. This religion contained all that was best in Stoicism and in Neo-Platonism, but with an animating principle of spiritual life absent in both. Roman literature said not a word of it. But while the learned were contemptuous and incredulous it was creeping into households and hearts and silently winning disciples throughout the empire. Stoicism itself had been unconsciously modified by it, and was in fact expiring when Marcus Aurelius was writing his profoundly religious *Meditations*. This philosopher had need of all his stoicism in his unhappy domestic relations, with his perverse and dissolute wife Faustina instigating rebellion in the east, and striving to win the love of Spartacus the gladiator, who was the idol of the hour in Rome; while his son and heir Commodus had no higher ambition than himself to enter the arena, after the fashion of many patrician youths of the period.

Chapter XI

The reign of Commodus is recognized as the beginning of the political decline of the empire. The loathsome vice and brutality of this son of the great moralist could not be written; and when he was strangled by one of his discarded favorites there was rejoicing in Rome. Of the twenty-five emperors who succeeded him ten were slain by their soldiers. It was the Praetorian Guards, after Commodus, who appointed the wearers of the Imperial purple, and if they might make emperors, they believed they might also unmake them, by slaying them, and when they commenced the practice of giving the throne to the highest bidder, political degradation could go no farther. The reign of Septimius Severus, which was a period of wholesome military despotism, is a relief. The wall he built in Britain still stands as his memorial. He died at York while engaged in this work, and there soon followed the reign of his son, Caracalla, of hideous memory (211-217 a.d.), whose first act was his one stroke of the pen to proscribe twenty thousand victims, because they wept for his brother and rival, Gaeta, over whose dead body he had climbed to the throne. We will not pause over the malignant cruelty of this being, who might have instructed Nero in the art; nor over Heliogabalus his successor (218-222 a.d.), of whom it was said, he could feel no appetite for his dinner, unless witnessing the shedding of human blood.

Under Decius (250-268 a.d.) the Christian persecutions were recommenced with greater severity than ever before. The early Christians had found an asylum in the catacombs of Rome; now again those vast subterranean corridors lined with tombs became the refuge and the abode of thousands of the hunted sect, traces of whom may still be found in the small mortuary chapels where they worshipped and sang their triumphant song — "Though He slay me, yet will I praise Him!"

While this was happening the Goths were invading the empire on its northern frontier, Persia hostile in the east, and also many small centres of rebellion in Asia were claiming independence. At Palmyra the learned and fascinating Zenobia, after the death of her husband, had reigned with great ability and splendor, assuming to be not alone Queen of Palmyra and Syria, but of the eastern division of the Roman Empire. It was under Aurelian (270-275 a.d.) that Palmyra fell after a long siege, and the fleeing queen was captured and carried to Rome, where she adorned the magnificent triumph. Fettered with gold chains, the proud captive walked before the triumphal car of her captor, who then gallantly bestowed upon her a splendid villa at Tivoli, where she dwelt in sumptuous retirement.

Rome no longer had the abounding vigor of her prime, when with her right hand she grasped Gaul, Spain, Africa, and Britain; and with her left gathered in all the fruits of Alexander's triumphs. Since the Goths had begun to press down upon her like a torrent; since she was defending, not extending her borders, she began to find that her life-current was not swift and strong enough to keep her distant provinces in subjection. Zenobia was not the only rebel against her authority. And if the Praetorian Guards in the West might create emperors, the legions in the East thought they also might do so. Anarchy and threatened dissolution led to an extraordinary measure, the decentralisation of authority. Diocletian, for administrative purposes, divided the empire into four parts (284), three other cities sharing the authority with Rome. Although this was only temporary, it presaged the end. The principle of unity was the life of Rome, and when that was impaired or abandoned, as it was soon to be, the empire might by ingenious devices be reinforced, and its existence prolonged, but the life of the organism was departing; its gigantic framework was beginning to weaken and to yield.

The Emperor having restored the integrity of the empire in the East, determined to complete his work by a less difficult task at home—the extirpation of that mischievous Christian sect which was spreading with astonishing rapidity. A systematic persecution was commenced. The one under Decius had been cruel, but it did not approach in severity this final effort to exterminate the new religion. But it was in vain. Panoplied in their sustaining faith, the ranks of the slain were immediately filled with men, women, and even children, who courted martyrdom as the open door to heaven; and when Diocletian became ill, and then abdicated, the attempt was abandoned.

Constantine succeeded him, first as joint ruler in the East with Licinius; but by the year 314 he was sole master of the empire. It is not probable that it was the caprice of a single man which converted the pagan empire into a Christian one. Here, in this strange faith, there existed a tremendous constructive force, an embodiment of unity, and of the associative principle. These had been the secret of the strength of Rome; and she was dissolving because she had lost them. There was a power in this Christianity which bound men together, not as by bands of steel, but as if by an irresistible, self-recruiting force of nature.

They could not destroy it, and so men wise in statesmanship doubtless saw the political expediency of adopting it. Whether Constantine had really learned to rely upon the God of the Christians, and whether he really saw a luminous cross in the heavens, who can tell? We only know that early in his reign the religion of the despised Nazarene was accepted by him, and the great Roman Empire became the standard-bearer of the Cross.

And when Constantine removed the seat of his empire to Byzantium, the newly christened city of Constantinople was the capital of a Christianized Roman Empire.

The Roman nation, sick and weary with a sense of moral degradation, embraced the new faith with rapture. Steeped to the lips in iniquity, they still might be cleansed! By the waters of baptism, though their sins were as scarlet, they might be made white as snow. A great wave of reaction carried men into asceticism, Rome fleeing to the deserts, there to find regeneration by austerities; and so in time monasticism was born.

The Apostolic Church had first been organized into communities under the rule of elders. In the second century, as it grew in numbers and in extent, there were created bishops, with a supervising care and an authority superior to that of the elders. From this nucleus started the organization of the Church of Rome. There were now bishops of Rome, and of Antioch, and of Alexandria. But as Peter when he perished at Rome was the head of the Apostolic Church, so the bishops of Rome were his successors, and had a precedence over the others. In this way, the hierarchy grew into form, and upon this historic relation to Peter, the founder of the Church, was based the claim of headship, which finally sundered the Greek and Roman churches.

A triumphant Christianity had entered through two doors. One was the heart of the people, the other a political door. To the great, the powerful, those who were going to control its destinies, the Christian faith meant a new source of strength for the empire. It was a coat of mail for its defence, and a weapon with which to smite its enemies. Emperors and their subordinates, fed and nourished on cruelty, were going to use the same ferocity in maintaining it that they had once used for its destruction. When historians express wonder that the gentle and persecuted Christians were so soon transformed into persecutors, they seem to forget that the faith of Christ was wrenched from the hands of His lowly followers and converted into an engine to be used for political ends. And one of the greatest miracles attending the history of Christianity is that so much of its purity and sanctity has survived this process of degradation. But however corrupt, however cruel, however perverted from its original simplicity in belief and form, there were always flowing, deep below the surface, uncontaminated streams of religious fervor; men and women with a faith as pure and as exalted as that of the first Disciples; for which they were ready, like them, to die. This miracle of divine persistence never tailed, and through ages of corruption has safely brought the living waters which nourish Christendom today.

A time of unprecedented overturnings was at hand. The Huns had appeared in Europe (375 A.D.), and, like wolves, were driving before them even the Goths, who poured down upon the Italian frontiers. It became evident that the western division of the empire, including Italy, Gaul, Spain, Africa, and Britain, could no longer be afforded protection by Constantinople. In 395 a.d. the dismemberment took place. There was an Eastern Empire and a Western Empire. The Eastern or Byzantine Empire, with comparative internal and external tranquillity, was going to stand in shining petrifaction for nearly a thousand years. But the Western Empire was crumbling—decay within and foes without. The Moors were threatening Africa, The Picts and Scots called for a strong hand in Britain, and most terrible of all, the Visigoths under Alaric were boldly invading northern Italy; besieging Milan, attacking Florence, then plundering, destroying, burning, as they made their way to the Eternal City. Never but once—600 years before—had foreign feet profaned the streets of Rome. Slaves within the city opened a gate to their kinsmen encamped without; and at midnight the awful moment arrived when, with a wild shout, the Goths were in Rome. The horrors of the sacking and the burning need not be dwelt upon.

The scattering of patrician families consequent upon this pillage and devastation, forever dispersed the traditional elements which made Rome so sacred. All of Italy was subject to the Visigoths, who were also in Gaul and in Spain, The Angles and the Saxons were in Britain, and the Vandals in Africa. Rome, herself almost submerged, saw the dark waters of this northern deluge flowing over the entire empire in the West.

The death of Alaric in 410, and the advent of Ataulf, his brother and successor, as head of the Visigoths, temporarily stayed the course of events. Ataulf loved and had carried away Plaeidia, sister of the recent Emperor Honorius. He was an admirer of Roman civilization, and approved of preserving it as a foundation for a Gothic structure, rather than destroying it. So he restored the empire in name, and withdrew with his Roman bride, Plaeidia, to Spain, there to found a Visigoth Empire. So for some decades longer emperors bearing the name, but with no actual power, flit like ghosts across the page of history, the barbarians deciding who should and who should not wear the imperial purple.

Rome was not defiled by the feet of Attila and his Huns, although they fiercely ravaged Italy. But the Vandals visited it with fire and with sword and insult. Genseric, following the lines of the old Carthaginian Empire, was creating a huge Vandal Empire, and was master of the Mediterranean—that prize for which ancient nations had once so fiercely struggled. He, with his Vandals and his Moors, visited Rome with destruction and degrading insult (455 A..D.), and after fourteen devastating days, they carried all the portable treasure to Carthage, leaving only what was rooted to the ground. This final humiliation extinguished the flickering spark of life in the expiring empire, and in 495 a.d. the Roman Senate performed its last act. It transferred the supreme authority to Odoacer, chief of a German tribe, and a Goth was King of Rome and Sovereign of Italy.

Made in the USA
Lexington, KY
22 June 2018